D1192216

Eyewitness Accounts of the American Revolution

Lieutenant James Moody's Narrative of his Exertions and Sufferings

The New York Times & Arno Press

Reprinted from a copy in the collections of
The New York Public Library
Astor, Lenox and Tilden Foundations

*

*

Library of Congress Catalog Card No. 67-29040

*

Manufactured in the U.S.A.

LIEUT. MOODY'S

NARRATIVE.

LIEUT. JAMES MOODY'S

NARRATIVE

OF HIS

EXERTIONS AND SUFFERINGS

IN THE

CAUSE OF GOVERNMENT,

Since the YEAR 1776;

AUTHENTICATED BY PROPER CERTIFICATES.

THE SECOND EDITION.

LONDON:

Printed; and fold by RICHARDSON and URQUHART, at the Royal Exchange; WILKIE, St. Paul's Church-Yard; FAULDER, Bond-Street; and S. HAYES, Oxford-Street.

MDCCLXXXIII.

LIEUTENANT MOODY'S

NARRATIVE, &c.

CHOICE and plan, it would ſeem, have ſeldom much influence in determining either men's characters, or their conditions. Theſe are uſually the reſult of circumſtances utterly without our controul. Of the truth of this poſition, the Writer's own recent hiſtory affords abundant proofs.

Seven years ago, few human events ſeemed more improbable, than that he, a plain, contented farmer, ſettled on a large, fertile, pleaſant, and well-improved farm of his own, in the beſt climate and happieſt country in the world, ſhould ever beat his plough-ſhare into a ſword, and commence a *ſoldier*. Nor was it leſs improbable that he ſhould ever become a *writer*, and be called upon to print a *narrative* of his own adventures. Yet neceſſity and a ſenſe of duty, contrary to his natural inclination, ſoon forced him to appear in

 the

the former of theſe characters; and the importunity of friends has now prevailed with him to aſſume the latter.

When the preſent ill-fated Rebellion firſt broke out, he was, as has already been hinted, a happy farmer, without a wiſh or an idea of any other enjoyment, than that of making happy, and being happy with, a beloved wiſe, and three promiſing children. He loved his neighbours, and hopes they were not wholly without regard for him. Clear of debt, and at eaſe in his poſſeſſions, he had ſeldom thought much of political or ſtate queſtions; but he felt and knew he had every poſſible reaſon to be grateful for, and attached to, that glorious Conſtitution to which he owed his ſecurity. The firſt great uneaſineſs he ever felt, on account of the Public, was when, after the proceedings of the firſt Congreſs were known, he foreſaw the imminent danger to which this Conſtitution was expoſed; but he was completely miſerable when, not long after, he ſaw it totally overturned.

The ſituation of a man who, in ſuch a dilemma, wiſhes to do right, is trying and difficult. In following the multitude, he was ſure of popular applauſe; this is always pleaſing; and it is too dearly bought only when a man gives up for it the approbation of his own conſcience. He foreſaw, in its fulleſt force, that torrent of reproach, inſult, and injury, which he was ſure to draw down on

himſelf

himſelf and his family, by a contrary conduct; nor does he wiſh to deny, that, for ſome time, theſe overawed and ſtaggered him. For himſelf he felt but little; but he had either too much or too little of the man about him, to bear the ſeeing of his neareſt and deareſt relatives diſgraced and ruined. Of the points in debate between the parent-ſtate and his native country, he pretended not to be a competent judge: they were ſtudiouſly ſo puzzled and perplexed, that he could come to no other concluſion, than that, however real or great the grievances of the Americans *might* be, rebellion was not the way to redreſs them. It required moreover but little ſkill to know, that rebellion is the fouleſt of all crimes; and that what was begun in wickedneſs muſt end in ruin. With this conviction ſtrong upon his mind, he reſolved, that there was no difficulty, danger, or diſtreſs, which, as an honeſt man, he ought not to undergo, rather than ſee his country thus diſgraced and undone. In ſpite therefore of incapacity, in ſpite of diſinclination—nay, in ſpite even of concern for his family—with the moſt ardent love for his country, and the warmeſt attachment to his countrymen, he reſolved to do any thing, and to be any thing, not inconſiſtent with integrity—to fight, to bleed, to die—rather than live to ſee the venerable Conſtitution of his country totally loſt, and his countrymen enſlaved. What the conſequences of this reſolution have been, it is the intention of the following pages to deſcribe.

The facts now to be related have many of them been occasionally published in the New York papers, but in a state so mutilated and imperfect, as rather to excite than gratify curiosity. They are here brought together under one view, in a connected narrative; and set down just as they happened. It is not pretended that all his adventures are here related, or that all the circumstances of those related are fully enumerated. It would be impolitic and dangerous for him to recount, at large, all his various stratagems; it would be barbarous and base, to divulge all the means by which he has sometimes effected his almost miraculous escapes. But were it otherwise, nothing can be farther from his aim, than to make a pompous display of any supposed merit of his own. As to the truth of his principal facts, he appeals to sundry certificates and affidavits now in his possession; nay, he farther appeals to every officer of every rank, who has either lately served, or is still serving, in America. Yet, after all, from the nature of the case, the credit of some parts of this Narrative must rest upon his own authority, which, he believes, will not be questioned by those who are acquainted with his character.

Of the true causes that gave birth to this unhappy quarrel, Mr. Moody is unwilling to give any opinion. He is no politician; and, therefore, by no means qualified to reconcile the contradictory assertions and arguments of the contending parties.

parties. This only, as an individual of that deſcription of people of whom the greateſt part of every community muſt conſiſt, he thinks it incumbent on him to declare, that it did not originate with the *people* of America, properly ſo called. They felt no real grievances, and therefore could have no inducement to riſk ſubſtantial advantages in the purſuit of ſuch as were only imaginary. In making this declaration, he is confident he ſpeaks the ſentiments of a great majority of the peaſantry of America. But, in every country, there are multitudes who, with little property, and perhaps ſtill leſs principle, are always diſpoſed, and always eager for a change. Such perſons are eaſily wrought upon, and eaſily perſuaded to enliſt under the banners of pretended patriots and forward demagogues; of whom alſo every country is ſufficiently prolific.

In America, theſe popular leaders had a ſet of men to aſſiſt them, who inherited, from their anceſtors, the moſt rooted diſlike and antipathy to the conſtitution of the parent-ſtate; and, by means of *their* friendly co-operation, they were able to throw the whole continent into a ferment in the year 1774, and maddened almoſt every part of the country with *Aſſociations*, *Committees*, and *Liberty-poles*, and all the preliminary apparatus neceſſary to a *Revolt*. The general cry was, *Join or die!* Mr. Moody reliſhed neither of theſe alternatives, and therefore remained on his farm a ſilent, but not

not unconcerned, ſpectator of the black cloud that had been gathering, and was now ready to burſt on his devoted head. It was in vain that he took every poſſible precaution, conſiſtent with a good conſcience, not to give offence. Some infatuated aſſociations were very near conſigning him to the latter of theſe alternatives, only becauſe neither his judgment, nor his conſcience, would ſuffer him to adopt the former. He was perpetually haraſſed by theſe Committees; and a party employed by them once actually aſſaulted his perſon, having firſt flouriſhed their *tomahawks* over his head in a moſt inſulting manner. Finding it impoſſible either to convince theſe aſſociators, or to be convinced by them, any longer ſtay among them was uſeleſs; and an attempt made upon him ſoon after, rendered it impoſſible. On Sunday 28th March 1777, while he was walking in his grounds with his neighbour Mr. Hutcheſon, he ſaw a number of armed men marching towards his houſe. He could have no doubt of their intention; and endeavoured to avoid them. They fired three different ſhots at him; but happily miſſed him, and he eſcaped. From this time, therefore, he ſought the earlieſt opportunity to take ſhelter behind the Britiſh lines; and ſet out for this purpoſe in April 1777. Seventy-three of his neighbours, all honeſt men, of the faireſt and moſt reſpectable characters, accompanied him in this retreat. The march was long and dangerous. They were repeatedly annoyed and aſſaulted;

ſaulted; and once they were under the neceſſity of coming to an engagement with a rebel party conſiderably ſuperior in number. Men, circumſtanced as he and his friends were, could want no arguments to animate their exertions. The attack was ſharp, but the Loyaliſts were ſucceſſful; the enemy gave way, leaving them at liberty to purſue their route unmoleſted. The whole company, four only excepted, arrived ſafe at Bergen, where they joined Lieutenant-colonel Barton's battalion, in General Skinner's brigade*. A few, whoſe profeſſions were calculated to render them uſeful in that department, joined the engineers.

In June following, Mr. Moody and Mr. *Hutcheſon*, went privately, about 70 miles into the country, to enliſt the friends of Government. They enliſted upwards of 500 men. The Britiſh army, then at Brunſwick, was expected immediately to march through New Jerſey. Mr. Moody and his friends had their agents properly placed, to give them the earlieſt information of the army's moving; when their plan was, to diſarm the diſaffected, and generally arm the Loyal. Let the Reader then judge of their mortification, when, whilſt their adherents were high in ſpirits, and confident of their ability, at one blow, as it were, to have cruſhed the Rebellion in New Jerſey, they were informed, that General Howe had evacuated the

* Vide General Skinner's Certificate.

province, and was gone to the ſouthward†. Notwithſtanding this diſcouragement, Mr. Moody and his party ſtill continued in the country agreeably to their inſtructions, in the hope that ſome opportunity would ſtill preſent itſelf to annoy the rebellious, and to aſſiſt the loyal. But no ſuch opportunity offering immediately, they ſoon received orders to join the army with the men they had enliſted, or could enliſt.

In conſequence of theſe inſtructions, they ſet forwards with about 100 Loyaliſts (not more than that number, from the change of proſpects, were then to be prevailed upon to leave their own country; or, if it had been otherwiſe, the time was too ſcanty, being not more than 48 hours to collect them together, which, it muſt be obvious, was to be done only with great caution and ſecrecy), on a march of upwards of 70 miles, through a well inhabited part of the province. The rebels purſued them; and, after ſeveral ſkirmiſhes, at length came upon them in ſuch force, near Perth-Amboy, that they were obliged to give way and diſperſe. More than ſixty of the party were taken priſoners; eight only, beſides Mr. Moody, got within the Britiſh lines. Theſe priſoners, after being confined in Morris town jail, were tried for what was called *high treaſon*;[b] and above one half of them were ſentenced to die. Two, whoſe names were *Iliff* and *Mee*, were

† This was to the Cheſapeak expedition.

actually

Sandy Hook to Shrewſbury. They eluded the vigilance of a Rebel Guard, and gained a place called *The Falls*. Here they ſurpriſed and took priſoners, one Colonel, one Lieutenant Colonel, one Major, and two Captains, with ſeveral other priſoners of inferior note; and, without injuring any private property, deſtroyed a conſiderable magazine of powder and arms. With theſe priſoners, and ſuch public ſtores as they were able to bring off, Mr. Hutcheſon was charged, whilſt Mr. Moody brought up the rear, with his ſixteen men, to defend them. They were, as they had expected, ſoon purſued by double their number, and overtaken. Mr. Moody kept up a ſmart fire on his aſſailants, checking and retarding them, till Mr. Hutcheſon, with their booty, had got a head to a conſiderable diſtance. He then alſo advanced, making for the next advantageous ſtation; and thus proceeded, from one good ſpot to another, ſtill covering the priſoners, till they had gained a ſituation on the ſhore at Black Point, where the enemy could not flank them. But, juſt at this time, the purſuers were reinforced with ten men: ſo that they were now forty ſtrong. Mr. Hutcheſon, with one man, croſſed the inlet, behind which he had taken ſhelter, and came to Mr. Moody's aſſiſtance: and now a warm engagement enſued, that laſted for three quarters of an hour. By this time all their ammunition, amounting to upwards of eighty rounds of cartridges, was expended; and ten men only, three of whom were wounded, were in any capacity to follow their leader to the charge. The bayonet was their only reſource; but this the enemy could not withſtand: they fled, leaving eleven of their number killed or wounded. Unfortunately, Mr. Moody's ſmall, but gallant, party could not follow up their blow; being, in a manner, utterly exhauſted by a long haraſſed march, in weather intenſely hot. They found the Rebel Captain dead, and their Lieutenant alſo expiring on the field. There was ſomething peculiarly ſhocking and awful in the death of the former. He was ſhot by Mr. Moody, whilſt, with the moſt bitter oaths and threats of vengeance, after having miſſed once, he was again levelling his piece at him. Soon after the engagement, one of the party came forwards, with an handkerchief flying from a ſtick, and demanded a parley. His ſignal was returned, ſignifying the willingneſs of the Loyaliſts to treat with him; and a truce was ſpeedily agreed on; the conditions of which were, That they ſhould have leave to take care of their dead and wounded; whilſt Mr. Moody's party was permitted, unmoleſted, to return to the Britiſh lines. Happily none of the wounds, which any of his men received in this expedition, proved mortal. The publick ſtores which they brought away with them, beſides thoſe which they had deſtroyed, ſold for upwards of five hundred pounds ſterling; and every ſhilling of this money was given by Mr. Moody to the men, as a ſmall reward for their very meritorious conduct.

About

About the middle of the October following, Mr. Moody was again ſent into the interior parts of the Rebel Country, to obtain intelligence reſpecting Waſhington's army. He ſucceeded; and his intelligence was communicated to General Pattiſon. Again, about the middle of November, he was deſired to find out the ſituation and circumſtances of an army under the Rebel General Sullivan, which had lately been on an expedition to the weſtward againſt the Indians. Accordingly, he went eighty miles into Pennſylvania, cloſe by Sullivan's camp; and obtained an exact account of the number of men and horſes with which he went out from Eaſton, on this Indian expedition; and the number alſo that he returned with.

From thence, he went to Morris County, where Waſhington then lay with his army. And here he had the good fortune to obtain, from their own books, an account of the rations which were drawn for them. He next went to Pumpton, where General Gates then was, on his march to the ſouthward; and here alſo he gained the exacteſt information, not only of the amount of the force then with him, but of the numbers that were expected to join him. And now, having pretty well gone through the buſineſs entruſted to him, he returned to New York, and continued there till next year.

In May 1780, he took with him four truſty men, and went into the Rebel Country, with the

intention

intention of ſurpriſing Governor Livingſton, a man whoſe conduct had been, in the moſt abandoned degree, cruel and oppreſſive to the loyal inhabitants of New Jerſey. When, with all neceſſary ſecrecy, Mr. Moody had got into his immediate neighbourhood, information was received, that Mr. Livingſton was gone to Trenton to meet the aſſembly; and that, on his return, he was to ſee ſome perſons on buſineſs at an appointed place. This made it neceſſary for the Enſign to alter his meaſures, as he did immediately. He led his party into Suſſex County, and there left them; himſelf only retiring to a proper ſituation, till his plan ſhould be ripe for execution. Being under a neceſſity of again returning into Suſſex, before any thing could be done, he had the mortification to find, that one of his men had been taken priſoner by a Rebel Major of the name of *Hoops*, who extorted a confeſſion from him that Moody was in the country, and, as he imagined, in queſt of ſome perſon of note, who lived near Morris Town. This blaſted the whole project; the intelligence was inſtantly ſent to Livingſton, who, too juſtly, concluded himſelf to be the perſon aimed at; and, of courſe, took every precaution to prevent a ſurpriſe.

Still, however, Mr. Moody flattered himſelf he ſhould yet be more fortunate, and do ſomething, notwithſtanding the alarm that was now ſpread through the country. The firſt plauſible

thing

thing that offered was, a plan to blow up the magazine at Suckasunna, about sixteen miles back of Morris Town; but this also proved abortive: for, notwithstanding his having prevailed on some British prisoners, taken with General Burgoyne, to join him in the enterprise, the alarm was now become so general, and the terror so great, that they had increased their guard around this magazine, to the number of an hundred and upwards; so that he was under the necessity of abandoning his project.

Returning again into Sussex County, he now heard that several prisoners were confined, on various suspicions and charges of loyalty, in the jail of that county; and that one of them was actually under sentence of death. This poor fellow was one of Burgoyne's soldiers, charged with crimes of a civil nature, of which, however, he was generally believed to be innocent. But when a clergyman of the Church of England interposed with his unrelenting prosecutor, and warmly urged this plea of innocence, he was sharply told, that, though he might not perhaps deserve to die for the crime for which he had been committed, there could be no doubt of his deserving to die, as an enemy to America. There was something so piteous, as well as shameful, in the case of this ill-fated victim to republican resentment, that it was determined, if possible, to release both him and his fellow-prisoners. For this purpose, Mr. Moody

Moody took with him ſix men; and, late at night, entered the country town, about ſeventy miles from New York. The inhabitants of the town were but too generally diſaffected. This ſuggeſted the neceſſity of ſtratagem. Coming to the jail, the keeper called out from the window of an upper room, and demanded what their buſineſs was? The Enſign inſtantly replied, "He had a priſoner "to deliver into his cuſtody." "What! One of "*Moody*'s fellows," ſaid the Jailor? "Yes," ſaid the Enſign. On his enquiring, what the name of this ſuppoſed priſoner was, one of the party, who was well known, by the inhabitants of that place, to be with Mr. Moody, perſonated the character of a priſoner, and ſpoke for himſelf. The jailor gave him a little ill language; but, notwithſtanding, ſeemed highly pleaſed with the idea of his having ſo notorious a Tory in his cuſtody. On the Enſign's urging him to come down, and take charge of the man, he peremptorily refuſed; alleging, that, in conſequence of Moody's being out, he had received ſtrict orders to open his doors to no man after ſun-ſet; and that therefore he muſt wait till morning. Finding that this tale would not take, the Enſign now changed his note; and, in a ſtern tone, told him, "Sirrah, the man who now ſpeaks to "you is Moody: I have a ſtrong party with me; "and, if you do not this moment deliver up "your keys, I will inſtantly pull down your houſe "about your ears." The jailor vaniſhed in a moment.

moment. On this, Mr. Moody's men, who were well ſkilled in the Indian war-whoop, made the air reſound with ſuch a variety of hideous yells, as ſoon left them nothing to fear from the inhabitants of New Town, which, though the country town, conſiſts only of twenty or thirty houſes. "The Indians "the Indians are come!"—ſaid the panic-ſtruck people: and happy were they who could ſooneſt eſcape into the woods. While theſe things were thus going on, the Enſign had made his way through a caſement, and was met by a priſoner, whom he immediately employed to procure him a light. The vaniſhed jailor was now again produced; and moſt obſequiouſly conducted Mr. Moody to the dungeon of the poor wretch under ſentence of death.

It may ſeem incredible, but it is an undoubted fact, that, notwithſtanding all the horrors and awfulneſs of his ſituation, this poor, forlorn, condemned Britiſh ſoldier was found faſt aſleep; and had ſlept ſo ſound, as to have heard nothing of the uproar or alarm. There is no poſſibility of deſcribing the agony of this man, when, on being thus ſuddenly arouſed, he ſaw before him a man in arms, attended by perſons, whom, though they were familiarly known to him, ſo agitated were his ſpirits, he was utterly at a loſs then to recognize. The firſt, and the only idea that occurred to him was, that, as many of the friends of Government had been privately executed in priſon,

 the

the perſon he ſaw was his executioner. On Mr. Moody's repeatedly informing him of his miſtake, and that he was come to releaſe him in the name of *King George*, the tranſition, from ſuch an abyſs of wretchedneſs to ſo extravagant a pitch of joy, had well nigh overcome him. Never before had the Writer been preſent at ſo affecting a ſcene. The image of the poor ſoldier, alternately agitated with the extremes of deſpair and rapture, is, at this moment, preſent to his imagination, as ſtrong almoſt as if the object were ſtill before him; and he has often thought, there are few ſubjects on which a painter of taſte and ſenſibility could more happily employ his pencil. The man looked wild; and undoubtedly was wild, and hardly in his ſenſes: and yet he laboured, and was big with ſome of the nobleſt ſentiments, and moſt powerful paſſions, by which the human mind is ever actuated. In ſuch circumſtances, it was with ſome difficulty that the Enſign got him away. At length, however, his clothes were got on; and he, with all the reſt who choſe to avail themſelves of the opportunity, were conducted into ſafety, notwithſtanding a warm purſuit of ſeveral days.

The humane reader, Mr. Moody perſuades himſelf, will not be leſs affected than he himſelf was, at the mournful ſequel of this poor ſoldier's tale. In the courſe of war he was again taken, and again conducted to the dungeon; and afterwards actually executed on the ſame ſentence on which

which he had been before convicted; though he left the world with the moſt ſolemn aſſeverations of his innocence, as to any crime of which he had been accuſed, excepting only an unſhaken allegiance to his Sovereign.

A few other particulars reſpecting this poor man, who, though but a common ſoldier in a marching regiment, was, in all the eſſential and beſt parts of the character, an hero, the Writer cannot excuſe himſelf from the relation of. His ſituation and circumſtances in the Rebel Country being peculiar, Mr. Moody, not thinking it proper himſelf to return thither ſo ſoon, took the earlieſt means he could to have him conveyed ſafe to New York. But no arguments, no intreaties, could prevail with him to leave his deliverer. "To "you," ſaid he, "I owe my life: to you, and in "your ſervice, let me devote it. You have found "me in circumſtances of ignominy: I wiſh for an "opportunity to convince you, that you have not "been miſtaken in thinking me innocent. I am, "and you ſhall find me, a good ſoldier." It was to this fatal, but fixed determination, that he ſoon after owed the loſs of his life.

When he was brought to the place of execution, the perſons, who had charge of him, told him, they had authority to promiſe him a reprieve; and they did moſt ſolemnly promiſe it to him, on condition

 only

only that he would tell them, who the Loyaliſts in the country were, that had aſſiſted Moody. His reply was moſt manly and noble; and proves, that real nobility and dignity of ſentiment are appropriated to no particular rank or condition of life. "I love life," he ſaid, "and there is nothing which a man of honour can do, that I "would not to do to ſave it; but I cannot pay this "price for it. The men you wiſh me to betray "muſt be good men, becauſe they have aſſiſted a "good man in a good cauſe. Innocent, as I am, "I feel this an awful moment: how far it becomes you to tempt me to make it terrible, by overwhelming me in the baſeſt guilt, "yourſelves muſt judge. My life is in your "power; my conſcience, I thank God, is ſtill "my own."

Another extraordinary circumſtance is ſaid to have befallen him; which, as well as the preceding, Mr. Moody relates on the teſtimony of an eye-witneſs yet living. Though he was a ſmall and light man; yet the rope, with which he was ſuſpended, broke. Even ſtill this poor man's admirable preſence of mind, and dignity of conſcious innocence, did not forſake him. He inſtantly addreſſed himſelf to the ſurrounding multitude, in the following words: "Gentlemen, I cannot but hope "that this very extraordinary event will convince "you, of what I again ſolemnly proteſt to you, "that I am innocent of the crime for which you

"have

" have adjudged me to die." But he ftill protefted in vain.

The fuppofed crime for which he fuffered was, the plundering and robbing the houfe of a certain furious and powerful Rebel. But it would be unjuft to his memory not to certify, as Mr. Moody does, that he has fince learned, from the voluntary confeffion of a lefs confcientious loyalift, that this honeft man was charged wrongfully; inafmuch as he himfelf, without the knowledge of the other, on the principles of retaliation and revenge, had committed the crime. The name of the abovementioned honeft foldier and martyr, was ROBERT MAXWELL, a Scotfman, who had had a good education.

Not long after, obtaining information of the Britifh army's moving towards Springfield, Mr. Moody concluded, that the campaign was open. There appeared no way in which, with his fmall party of feven men, he could be more ufeful, than by fecuring as many as he could of the Rebel Militia. Accordingly, it was not long before he contrived to take prifoners, a Major, a Captain, two Lieutenants, and fundry Committee Men; in all to the amount of eighteen. Some requefted to be parolled; and the Enfign complied with their requeft; becaufe it was not only reafonable and humane, but becaufe alfo it left him at liberty to purfue frefh objects. Some requefted

to

to take the oath of neutrality; and it was not lefs willingly adminiftered to them.

The Rebel part of the country was now again in an alarm; and the Enfign was again purfued and fought, according to the ftrong expreffion of Scripture, "as a partridge in the mountains." But "wandering in deferts, and in mountains, "and in dens and caves of the earth," by the bleffing of God, he ftill eluded all their refearches. At length, however, being under a neceffity of returning to New York, he collected a few more of Burgoyne's men; and, having now augmented his party to thirteen, he fet out for that capital. But his former good fortune now forfook him; and he himfelf was foon doomed to feel all thofe bitter calamities, from which it had been the object of his exertions to extricate others.

On the 21ft of July 1780, it was his ill hap to fall in with an army, which the Rebel General *Wayne* was conducting to the fiege of *The Block-houfe*, commanded by Captain *Ward*. Refiftance was vain, and retreat impracticable. Mr. Moody, and the greater part of his men, were now obliged to fubmit to captivity.

He, and two of his men, were immediately fent to a place called *The Slote*; where they were confined, with their hands tied behind their backs. On the 22d, they were removed to *Stony Point*; and,

and, on the 23d, to Colonel Robertſon's houſe, at *Weſt-Point*. The Rebel General *Howe*, who commanded at this poſt, treated Mr. Moody with great civility; and permitted his ſervant to attend him. From thence, he was ſent to *Fiſh-kill*, to the Rebel Commiſſary of priſoners, who paſſed him on to *Æſopus*. At *Æſopus*, he remained till the 2d of Auguſt; when, in the night, he was put into a ſtrong room, guarded by four ſoldiers, two within the door, and two without. The Serjeant, in the hearing of the Enſign, gave orders to the ſentinels who were in the room with him, to inſiſt on his lying down on a bed, and inſtantly to ſhoot him if he attempted to riſe from it. On this, he requeſted and inſiſted to ſee the Commiſſary. The Commiſſary came; and was aſked, if theſe orders were from him? His anſwer was, "The Serjeant "had done his duty; and he hoped the men "would obey their orders." Mr. Moody remonſtrated, and urged, that it was no uncommon thing with him to riſe from his bed in his ſleep: he requeſted therefore only, that, if he ſhould happen now to be overtaken with ſuch an infirmity, the men might be ordered to call him by his name, and at leaſt to awake him before they fired. All the anſwer he could obtain, from this tyrant-minion of tyrant-maſters, was a cool and moſt cutting repetition of his former words.

After having twice more changed the place of his confinement, on the 10th of Auguſt he was carried back to *Weſt-point*. And here his ſufferings ſeemed to be but beginning; for the cruelties he experienced, under the immediate eye of General *Arnold*, who then commanded there, infinitely exceeded all that he has ever met with before or ſince.

Nothing can be further from Mr. Moody's wiſhes than to become any man's accuſer; but no man ſhould be afraid either to hear, or to tell the truth, which is of no party, and ſhould be obſerved by all. Humanity, morever, is ſo lovely and neceſſary a virtue, and eſpecially in times of civil war, that Mr. Moody owns he is proud, and loves, to acknowledge and to praiſe it, even in an enemy; of courſe, he muſt lament and reprobate the want of it, though in his beſt friend. Under new maſters, it is hoped, General Arnold has learned new maxims. Compelled by truth, however, Mr. Moody muſt bear him teſtimony, that he was *then* faithful to his employers, and abated not an iota in fulfilling both the letter and the ſpirit of their general orders and inſtructions.

Mr. Moody feels this to be an unpleaſant part of his Narrative. It is with pain he purſues it. May it be permitted him then to give the ſubſequent part of it in the words of an affidavit, taken in the Judge Advocate's Office at New York, from the mouth of William Buirtis, who was confined for his loyalty in the ſame priſon with Mr. Moody.

" Judge-Advocate's Office,

" *New York*, *May* 11, 1782.

" THIS day perſonally appeared William " Buirtis, a Refugee from the county of Weſt " Cheſter, in the province of New-York, but now " reſiding on York Iſland, in the province aforeſaid; and, being duly ſworn on the Holy " Evangeliſts of Almighty God, depoſeth and " ſaith;

" That ſome time in the month of Auguſt " 1780, he (the deponent) was confined in a dungeon at Weſt Point Fort, under ſentence of " death, having been charged with giving certain " intelligence and information to General Mathew, " one of his Britannic Majeſty's Generals ſerving " at that time in America; that, about the middle " of the month of Auguſt aforeſaid, Lieutenant " *James Moody*, of Brigadier General Skinner's " firſt batallion, was brought under guard, and " confined in the ſame dungeon with him (the deponent); that, the day following, he (Lieutenant Moody) was put in irons and hand-cuffed; " that the hand-cuffs were of a particular ſort and " conſtruction, *ragged on the inſide* next the wriſt,

" which raggedneſs cauſed his wriſts to be much " cut and ſcarified; that ſoon after he (Lieute- " tenant Moody) was ironed and hand-cuffed, an " officer came and demanded his money, ſaying, " *he was ordered to take what money he had, and* " *ſhould obey his orders punctually*;" that the money " was not delivered, as he (Lieutenant Moody) " was reſolute in refuſing, and determined not to " give it up. He (Lieutenant Moody) then peti- " tioned General Benedict Arnold, at that time in " the Rebel ſervice, and Commanding Officer at " Weſt Point, to grant him relief; in which pe- " tition he ſet forth the miſerable ſituation he was " in, as alſo the torment he ſuffered, occaſioned " by the hand-cuffs; to which petition he received " no anſwer, though he was told, by two officers " in the Rebel ſervice, his petition had been deli- " vered to General Arnold.

" That about a week after his firſt petition had " been ſent, he petitioned a ſecond time for relief " from his ſuffering, requeſting moreover to be " brought to a trial, obſerving, that if he ſhould " be found guilty of death he ſhould deſire to ſuf- " fer, as death was much preferable to torment, " and being murdered by inches. Some little time " after the delivery of the ſecond petition, one of " General Arnold's Aids de Camps, whoſe name " he (the deponent) cannot recollect, came to the " dungeon; and, on ſeeing him (Lieutenant

" Moody),

" Moody), aſked, if that was the *Moody* whoſe " name was a terror to every good man? On " his replying that his name was Moody, he (the " Aid de Camp) replied in a ſcoffing manner, " *You have got yourſelf into a pretty ſituation*;" on " his (Lieutenant Moody's) ſaying the ſituation " was diſagreeable, but he hoped it would not " be of long continuance; he anſwered, he be- " lieved not, as he would ſoon meet with juſtice " (pointing at the ſame time to a gallows that was " erected in the ſight and view of the dungeon); " and alſo added, *there* is the gallows ready " erected, which he (meaning Moody) had long " merited. Lieutenant Moody anſwered, he made " no doubt he (the Aid de Camp) wiſhed to " ſee every Loyal Subject hanged, but he thanked " God, the power was not in *him*; but if he " (Lieutenant Moody) was hanged, it could be " for no other reaſon than being a Loyal Subject " to one of the beſt of Kings, and under one of " the beſt of Governments; and added, if he " had *ten* lives to loſe, he would ſooner forfeit the " ten as a Loyal Subject, than *one* as a Rebel; " and alſo ſaid, he hoped to live to ſee him (the " Aid de Camp), and a thouſand ſuch other vil- " lains, hanged for being Rebels. The officer " then ſaid he was ſent to examine his irons, as " he (Lieutenant Moody) had been frequently " troubling General Arnold with his petitions. " On examining the irons, he ſaid *they were too* " *bad*; and aſked, who put them on?—ſaying,

" *Irons were intended for ſecurity, not for torment*; " *but if any one merited such irons, he* (Lieutenant " Moody) *did in his opinion.* Lieutenant Moody, " however, was not relieved at that time from his " irons; but, about a week or ten days afterwards, " an officer came from General Waſhington, or- " dered the irons to be taken off, and Lieutenant " Moody to be better treated. In conſequence " of General Waſhington's order, he was better " uſed: that he (the deponent) knows no- " thing farther that happened, as he (Lieutenant " Moody), in a few days afterwards, was removed " from that place.

" WILLIAM BUIRTIS.

" Sworn before me at the time and place above " mentioned,

" RICHARD PORTER,
" Aſ. D^y. Judge-Advocate."

The above-mentioned dungeon was dug out of a rock, and covered with a platform of planks badly jointed, without any roof to it; and all the rain which fell upon it immediately paſſed through, and lodged in the bottom of this diſmal manſion. It had no floor but the natural rock; and the water, with the mud and filth collected, was commonly ankle-deep in every part of it. Mr. Moody's bed was an old door, ſupported by four ſtones,

ſtones, ſo as juſt to raiſe it above the ſurface of the water. Here he continued near four weeks; and, during moſt of the time, while he was tormented with irons in the manner mentioned above, no food was allowed him but ſtinking beef, and rotten flour, made up into balls or dumplins, which were thrown into a kettle and boiled with the meat, and then brought to him in a wooden bowl which was never waſhed, and which contracted a thick cruſt of dough, greaſe, and dirt. It is a wonder that ſuch air, and ſuch food, to ſay nothing of the wounds upon his legs and wriſts, were not fatal to him, eſpecially as the clothes on his back were ſeldom dry, and at one time were continually wet for more than a week together. After Mr. Waſhington interfered he was ſerved with wholeſome proviſions, and he was allowed to purchaſe for himſelf ſome milk and vegetables.

The ways of Providence are often myſterious, frequently bringing about its ends by the moſt unlikely means. To this inhuman treatment in General Arnold's camp, Mr. Moody owed his future ſafety. On the 1ſt of September he was carried to Waſhington's camp, and there confined near their Liberty-pole. Colonel *Skammel*, the Adjutant General, came to ſee him put in irons. When they had hand-cuffed him, he remonſtrated with the Colonel, deſiring that his legs, which were indeed in a worſe ſituation than even his wriſts, might be

examined;

examined; farther adding only, that death would be infinitely preferable to a repetition of the torments he had juſt undergone. The Colonel did examine his legs; and, on ſeeing them, he alſo acknowledged, that his treatment had indeed been too bad; and aſked, if General Arnold had been made acquainted with his ſituation. Mr. Moody feels a ſincere pleaſure in thus publicly acknowledging his obligations and his gratitude to Colonel Skammel, who humanely gave orders to the Provoſt Marſhal to take good care of him, and by no means to ſuffer any irons to be put on his legs, till they were likely to prove leſs diſtreſſing.

Mr. Moody attended the rebel army in its march over the *New Bridge*; and had an opportunity of obſerving their whole line, and counting their artillery. Every thing ſeemed ſmooth and fair; and he felt himſelf much at eaſe, in the proſpect of being ſoon exchanged; when, very unexpectedly, he was viſited by an old acquaintance, one of their Colonels, who informed him, that he was in two days time to be brought to trial; that *Livingſton* was to be his proſecutor, and that the Court Martial was *carefully picked* for the purpoſe. He ſubjoined, that he would do well to prepare for eternity, ſince, from the evidence which he knew would be produced, there was but one iſſue of the buſineſs to be expected. Mr. Moody requeſted to be informed, what it was the purpoſe of this evidence to prove? it was, his wellwiſher told him,

him, that he had aſſaſſinated a Captain Shaddock and a Lieutenant Hendrickſon. Theſe were the two officers who had fallen fairly in battle near Black Point, as has been already related. The Enſign replied, that he felt himſelf much at eaſe on that account, as it could be ſufficiently cleared up by their own people, who had been in, and had ſurvived, the *action*, as well as by ſome of their officers, who were at the time priſoners to him, and ſpectators of the whole affair. "All "this," ſaid his friend, "will be of little avail: "you are ſo obnoxious; you have been, and are "likely to be, ſo *miſchievous* to us, that, be "aſſured, we are reſolved to get rid of you at any "rate. Beſides, you cannot deny, and it can be "proved by inconteſtible evidence, that you have "enliſted men, in this *State*, for the King's ſer-"vice, and this, by our laws, is *death*."

Enſign Moody affected an air of unconcern at this information; but it was too ſerious and important to him to be really diſregarded; he reſolved, therefore, from that moment, to effect his eſcape, or to periſh in the attempt.

Every precaution had been taken to ſecure the place in which he was confined. It was nearly in the centre of the rebel camp. A ſentinel was placed within the door of his priſon, and another without, beſides four others cloſe round, and within a few yards of the place. The time now came on when

when he muſt either make his attempt, or loſe the opportunity for ever. On the night, therefore, of the 17th of September, buſy in ruminating on his project, he had, on the pretence of being cold, got a watch-coat thrown acroſs his ſhoulders, that he might better conceal, from his unpleaſant companion, the operations which he meditated againſt his hand-cuffs. While he was racking his invention, to find ſome poſſible means of extricating himſelf from his fetters, he providentially caſt his eye on a poſt faſtened in the ground, through which an hole had been bored with an auger; and it occurred to him that it might be poſſible, with the aid of this hole, to break the bolt of his hand-cuffs. Watching the opportunity, therefore, from time to time, of the ſentinel's looking another way, he thruſt the point of the bolt into the above-mentioned hole, and by cautiouſly exerting his ſtrength, and gradually bending the iron backwards and forwards, he at length broke it. Let the reader imagine what his ſenſations were, when he found the manacles drop from his hands! He ſprung inſtantly paſt the interior ſentinel, and ruſhing on the next, with one hand he ſeized his muſquet, and with the other ſtruck him to the ground. The ſentinel within, and the four others who were placed by the fence ſurrounding the place of his confinement, immediately gave the alarm; and, in a moment, the cry was general—"*Moody* is eſcaped "from the Provoſt." It is impoſſible to deſcribe the uproar which now took place throughout the whole camp. In a few minutes every man was in a buſtle; every man was looking for Moody, and multitudes paſſed him on all ſides—little ſuſpecting, that a man whom they ſaw deliberately marching along, with a muſket on his ſhoulder, could be the fugitive they were in queſt of. The darkneſs of the night, which was alſo bluſtering and drizzly, prevented any diſcrimination of his perſon, and was indeed the great circumſtance that rendered his eſcape poſſible.

But no ſmall difficulty ſtill remained to be ſurmounted. To prevent deſertion, which at that time, was very frequent, Waſhington had ſurrounded his camp with a chain of ſentinels, poſted at about forty or fifty yards diſtance from each other; he was unacquainted with their ſtations; to paſs them undiſcovered was next to impoſſible; and to be diſcovered would certainly be fatal. In this dilemma Providence again befriended him. He had gained their ſtation without knowing it, when luckily he heard the watch-word paſſed from one to another—"Look ſharp to the chain—Moody is "eſcaped from the Provoſt." From the ſound of the voices he aſcertained the reſpective ſituations of theſe ſentinels; and, throwing himſelf on his hands and knees, he was happy enough to crawl through the vacant ſpace between two of them, unſeen by either. Judging that their line of purſuit would naturally be towards the Britiſh army, he made a detour into the woods on the oppoſite ſide. Through theſe woods he made as much ſpeed as the darkneſs of the night would permit, ſteering his courſe, after the Indian manner, by occaſionally groping and feeling the *white-oak*. On the ſouth ſide the bark of this tree is rough and unpleaſant to the touch, but on the north ſide it is ſmooth; hence it ſerves the ſagacious traverſer of the deſart, by night as well as by day, for his compaſs. Through the moſt diſmal woods and ſwamps he continued to wander till the night of the 21ſt, a ſpace of more than fifty-ſix hours during which time, he had no other ſuſtenance than a few *beach* leaves (which, of all that the woods afforded, were the leaſt unpleaſant to the taſte, and leaſt pernicious to health), which he chewed and ſwallowed, to abate the intolerable cravings of his hunger.

In every inhabited diſtrict he knew there were friends of Government; and he had now learned alſo where and how to find them out, without endangering *their* ſafety, which was always the firſt object of his concern. From ſome of theſe good men he received minute information how the purſuit after him was directed, and where every guard was poſted. Thus aſſiſted, he eluded their keeneſt vigilance; and, at length, by God's bleſſing, to his unſpeakable joy, he arrived ſafe at *Paulus-Hook*.

On the 6th of March 1781, Colonel Delancey, the Adjutant General, requeſted Mr. Moody to make

make an expedition into the rebel country, for the purpoſe of intercepting Mr. Waſhington's diſpatches. He readily conſented; and ſet out on the expedition the very next night, and travelled about twenty-five miles. The following day he and his party kept concealed in a ſwamp. The next night, for it was only by night that they could venture to ſtir, they had not gone far, when the man who had undertaken to be their guide, refuſed to advance a ſtep further. No arguments, no promiſes, no threats, could prevail with him to proceed, though it was at his own expreſs deſire that he was one of the party. Incenſed at his being ſo perverſe and wrong-headed, Mr. Moody, in the firſt tranſports of indignation, had actually cocked his gun in order to ſhoot him; but happily he inſtantly recollected, that the poor devil had a wife and family who depended on him for bread. This reſtrained him; and ordering his arms to be taken from him, he was under the painful neceſſity of returning with him to New York.

This man was remarkably earneſt and vehement in his reſentment againſt the Rebels. He had been much injured by them in his property; and they had alſo put both his father and his brother to an ignominious death. It was natural to ſuppoſe, therefore, that ſuch a man would be true and firm. But he was loyal only through reſentment and intereſt, not from conviction and principle. Theſe

Loyalifts, from principle, were the men on whom he relied; and no one of thefe ever failed him.

The Adjutant General feemed to be much difappointed on feeing the party return, fuppofing the hope of obtaining the difpatches to be now vain. Mr. Moody informed him of what had happened; but added, that he had ever fince kept his eye on the renegado, and had not fuffered a foul to fpeak to him; and requefted that this caution fhould be ftill continued, and that even the fentry, who was to guard him, fhould not be permitted to have any intercourfe with him. *On this condition* he promifed again to make the attempt, and hoped not without fuccefs. Accordingly, he fet out a fecond time; and, on the night of the 10th, he reached Haverftraw mountains. On his march he was informed, that the poft had gone by that day. On the 11th the weather became very inclement, and he, with his party, fuffered exceedingly from a heavy fall of fnow; notwithftanding, they pufhed forward, hoping, by rapid marches, to get a-head of the rider. Thefe efforts, though exceffively fatiguing, were as yet all in vain; but on the 15th they were fuccefsful, and got poffeffion of their prize; and, after fome equally difficult and diftreffing marches on their return, they at length arrived fafe with it in New York. The inexpreffible hardfhips which the party underwent in this adventure, both from hunger and cold, were

fatal

fatal to the health of moſt of them. Soon after Mr. Moody was made a Lieutenant, having firſt ſerved more than a year as a volunteer without any pay, and almoſt three years as an Enſign.

About the middle of May the Adjutant General again complained of the want of intelligence, and told Lieutenant Moody, that he could not render the King's cauſe a more eſſential piece of ſervice than by bringing in, if it were poſſible, another rebel mail. There was no declining ſuch a ſolicitation. Therefore, on the night of the 15th, taking four men with him, Mr. Moody ſet out, and travelled twenty-five miles. Hitherto he and his aſſociates met with no moleſtation; but they had not gone far the next night, when they perceived a conſiderable party of men approaching them as ſecretly as poſſible. Mr. Moody tried to get off by the left, but he found himſelf and his party incloſed on three ſides. On the right was a high cliff of rocks, ſo rugged and ſteep that the enemy thought it impoſſible for them to eſcape on that ſide. It was obvious, from theſe circumſtances, that an ambuſh was laid, and that this ſpot, ſo peculiarly convenient, was choſen for the purpoſe; in ſhort, that Mr. Moody and his party had been betrayed by intelligence ſent forward from New York. The only alternative left was to ſurrender and periſh, or to leap down from the top of theſe rocks, without knowing, with any certainty, either how high they were, or what ſort of ground was at the bottom. The Lieutenant bade his men follow him, and ſprang forward. Providentially the ground at the bottom was ſoft, and every thing elſe juſt as they could have wiſhed it: they eſcaped unhurt, and proceeded for ſome time unmoleſted. But, at no great diſtance, croſſing a ſwamp, juſt beyond it they fell in with another party, of much the ſame number as the former. Luckily they ſaw, and were not ſeen. A little hillock was at hand, to which the Lieutenant ordered his men quietly to retreat, and fall on their faces; judging that, in caſe they were diſcovered, there would be ſome advantage in having to charge from higher ground, by which means, if at all, they might cut their way through the party. What he and his men felt, when they beheld ſo ſuperior a force marching directly towards them, till at laſt they were within fifty yards; or when, in this awful moment, they had the happineſs to ſee them. without being diſcovered, take another courſe; no perſon of ſenſibility will need to be told. A little council of war was now held, and it was determined to return whither only the way ſeemed clear. To advance was impracticable, as there now could remain not a doubt but that intelligence of the intended route had been ſent from within the Britiſh lines, and that the enemy had made a proper uſe of it. They began, therefore, with all poſſible caution, to meaſure back their ſteps; for they were ſtill apprehenſive of other plots and other ambuſhes.

And

And now, having gained the North River, and being within four miles of New York, they flattered themſelves they were once more out of danger. But, being within a hundred yards of a certain houſe, how were they alarmed when they ſaw ſeventy men come out of it, and advance directly towards them! Lieutenant Moody was convinced they were Rebels; but the guide inſiſted that they were Loyaliſts, and that he *knew* ſeveral of them. On this, the latter, with another man, went forward to meet them, notwithſtanding that the former ſtill perſiſted in his opinion. A very unpleaſant ſalute ſoon convinced this unfortunate *duumvirate* of their miſtaken confidence. The main body made for the Lieutenant, who had no other means of eſcape than to climb a ſteep hill; but, long before he had reached the ſummit, they had ſo gained on him as to be within fifty yards. He received one general diſcharge, and thought it little ſhort of a miracle that he eſcaped unwounded. The bullets flew like a ſtorm of hail all around him; his clothes were ſhot through in ſeveral places; one ball went through his hat, and another grazed his arm. Without at all ſlackening his pace he turned round, and diſcharged his muſquet, and by this ſhot killed one of his purſuers: ſtill they kept up their fire, each man diſcharging his piece as faſt as he could load; but, gaining an opportunity of ſoon doubling upon them, he gave them the ſlip, and in due time arrived, once more, ſafe in New York. One of the two men who had

eſcaped,

eſcaped, and got in firſt, miſtaking the ſcreams of the poor fellow who was ſhot, for thoſe of Lieutenant Moody himſelf, had given out that the Lieutenant was killed, for that he had heard his cries; but the friends of the latter were ſoon happy to ſee ſo unequivocal a proof that the man was miſtaken.

The very firſt night after his return to New York, as above related, *viz.* on the 18th of May, Lieutenant Moody ſet out again on the buſineſs of this expedition. The Rebels knew that he had been driven back, and he thought it the propereſt time to proceed immediately in purſuit of his object. On that night, with his ſmall party of four men, he got as far as Secaucas. The next night they croſſed the Hackinſack river, by means of a canoe which Lieutenant Moody always kept there for ſuch purpoſes, and which, after croſſing, he concealed till his return. He then proceeded on, till, coming to the edge of a marſh, he fell in with a party of Rebels, who were patrolling in that quarter, with a view only, it is probable, of intercepting the country people who might be carrying proviſions to New York. This party diſcovered the Lieutenant firſt, without being ſeen, and ſuffered him to paſs their van, not hailing him till ſome of them were in his rear, as well as ſome in his front. He was ordered inſtantly to *ſtand*, or he and all with him were dead men. This ſummons the Lieutenant anſwered by an immediate

5 diſcharge,

diſcharge, which they returned. He then calling on his rear to advance, as if he had a large body in reſerve, and giving a ſecond fire, they ſoon diſperſed. He was informed the next day, that this rebel party conſiſted of twelve men.

Marching on about four miles farther, he came to Saddle River, which it was neceſſary to croſs; but apprehenſive that there might be a guard ſtationed at the bridge, though the night was diſmally dark and rainy, and the river had greatly overflowed its banks, he waded, for ſeveral yards, through a conſiderable depth of water, till he got cloſe to the bridge, where he ſaw, as he had feared, a regular guard. On this he retreated with all poſſible ſpeed and caution; and was obliged to wade through the river, about half a mile farther up, not without much difficulty and danger.

The country being now much alarmed with rumours of Moody's being out, occaſioned by this little rencontre, the *mail*, inſtead of being ſent by Pompton, as it uſually had been, and where it was expected to be met with, was now ſent by the back road, with a guard to ſecure it. On diſcovering this, the Lieutenant diſpatched a truſty Loyaliſt to a diſtant part of the province, with letters to his friends; and particularly directing one of them, whoſe perſon, figure, and voice moſt reſembled his own, to paſs for him but a ſingle hour; which he readily did. In this friend's neighbourhood lived a pompous and important Juſtice of a Peace, who was a cowardly fellow, and of courſe had been cruel. At this man's houſe, early in the evening, the perſon employed raiſed an alarm. The Juſtice came out, and eſpying, as it was intended he ſhould, *a tall man*, his fears convinced him it was Moody; and he inſtantly betook himſelf to the woods. The next day the rumour was general, that Moody was in that part of the country: and the militia was brought down from the part where he really was, to purſue him where he was not. This facilitated the capture of the *mail*, which he waylaid for five days before the opportunity preſented. This mail contained all the diſpatches that were ſent in conſequence of the interview between General Waſhington and the Count Rochambeau in Connecticut.[a]

Lieutenant Moody cauſed two other mails to be taken by the people under his direction. In one of theſe little expeditions his brother commanded, a young man, whoſe fearleſs courage, in the very teeth of danger, he had repeatedly witneſſed. The younger Moody ſucceeded in his attempt, ſo far as to intercept the mail; but, after ſeizing it, he was attacked by a ſuperior party, and two of his men were taken; yet he himſelf had the good fortune to eſcape, with that part of the papers which was in his own cuſtody. Pennſylvania was the ſcene of this enterpriſe.

A tale

A tale far more melancholy than any yet related comes now to be told; the recollection of which (and it is impoſſible he ſhould ever forget it) will for ever wring with anguiſh the heart of the Writer of this Narrative. In the end of October 1781, Major Beckwith, Aid de Camp to General Knip-hauſen, came and informed Lieutenant Moody, that one *Addiſon* had been with him, on a project of high moment. It was nothing leſs than to bring off the moſt important books and papers of Congreſs. This Addiſon was an Engliſhman; and had been employed in ſome inferior department, under Mr. Thompſon, the Secretary to the Congreſs. He was then a priſoner; and the plan was, that he ſhould be immediately exchanged, return in the uſual manner to Philadelphia, and there reſume his old employment. The Lieutenant was abundantly careful, and even ſcrupulous, in his inquiries concerning the man's character; on which head Major Beckwith expreſſed the moſt entire confidence; and obſerved, that Addiſon was equally cautious reſpecting the characters of thoſe who were to attend him.

The matter was of importance; and Lieutenant Moody was confident that, though it might be difficult to perform his part of the buſineſs, yet it was not impracticable. He reſolved, however, as Addiſon might think *him* an object worth betraying, that he ſhould not be informed of his conſenting to be of the party. If any other perſon did inform him of it, he was, to ſay the leaſt, very imprudent. The Lieutenant pitched upon his only brother, of whom ſome mention has already been made, and another faithful American ſoldier, for this arduous enterpriſe. Their firſt inſtructions were to wait on Addiſon, and to bind him, as they themſelves had juſt been bound, to mutual ſecrecy and fidelity, by an *oath*, which the Lieutenant had always adminiſtered to his followers in all his expeditions, when the importance of the object rendered ſuch an additional tie neceſſary ; and which, as it clearly ſhews the principles of honour and humanity on which it was his uniform pride and purpoſe to act, he begs leave here to ſubjoin, and it as follows ; *viz.*

" I, the underſigned A. B. do ſolemnly ſwear, " on the Holy Evangeliſts of Almighty God, that " I will ſtand by and be true to the perſons joined " with me in this expedition, and do every thing " in my power to accompliſh the purpoſes of it : " and I do farther ſwear, that, in caſe of our tak- " ing any priſoners, I will do my endeavour to " treat them as well as our ſituation will admit of : " and I do farther ſwear, that, in caſe any acci- " dent ſhould happen to me, and that I ſhould " be taken, I will not, even to ſave life, diſcover " or betray any perſon joined with me, or any " Loyaliſt who may befriend us with any informa- " tion, advice, or other aſſiſtance ; and I do far- " ther ſwear, that I will not injure nor deſtroy any

" property

" property even of a rebel, unleſs it be arms or
" ammunition, but faithfully pay the full price of
" any thing we take from them, if they refuſe to
" ſell it: and I do farther ſwear, that I will not
" wound nor take away the life of any perſon
" whatever, unleſs they ſhould attempt an eſcape
" when in our cuſtody, or it ſhall otherwiſe be ab-
" ſolutely neceſſary for our own defence. *So help*
" *me God.*"

After taking this oath, a certain number of nights was agreed on, in which Addiſon was to expect them; and a certain place alſo appointed, where he was to meet them. In ſuch an adventure, it was impoſſible to be exact to any time; but it was agreed, that if they failed of being at the place in any of the ſpecified nights, he ſhould no longer expect them; and they farther promiſed, by proper means, to appriſe him, if poſſible, if any accident ſhould befal them, ſo as either to delay, or wholly put an end to their project.

Things being thus ſettled, Addiſon left New York in due form and manner, as was generally ſuppoſed, in order to return to his former friends and employment; and, at the proper time, Lieutenant Moody and his friends followed him. The manner and circumſtances of their march, it is not material nor proper here to relate: Suffice it to ſay, that, on the night of the 7th of November, the firſt in the order of thoſe that had been appointed,

pointed, they arrived in the neighbourhood of Philadelphia, but on the oppoſite ſide of the river. They found Addiſon already on the ſpot, waiting for them, according to appointment. Lieutenant Moody kept a little back, at ſuch a diſtance as not to have his perſon diſtinguiſhed, yet ſo as to be within hearing of the converſation that paſſed. His brother, and *Marr* his aſſociate, on going up to Addiſon, found him apparently full of confidence, and in high ſpirits; and every thing ſeemed to promiſe ſucceſs. He told them, that their plot was perfectly ripe for execution; that he had ſecured the means of admiſſion into the moſt private receſſes of the State-houſe, ſo that he ſhould be able the next evening to deliver to them the papers they were in queſt of. They, on their parts, aſſured him, that every neceſſary precaution had been taken to ſecure and expedite their retreat; and that they had with them *a ſure friend*, who would wait for them on that ſide of the river, who, as well as themſelves, would die by his ſide, rather than deſert him, ſhould any diſaſter befal them. He replied, that they ſhould find *him* as true and faithful to them and their cauſe, as they themſelves could poſſibly be. Soon after they croſſed the river together to Philadelphia; and it is probable that, on the paſſage, Addiſon was for the firſt time informed, that this friend was Lieutenant Moody. Whether it was this diſcovery that put it firſt into his head, or whether he had all along intended it, and had already taken the neceſſary previous ſteps, the Lieutenant cannot certainly ſay; but he aſſures himſelf, that every generous-minded man will be ſhocked when he reads, that this perfidious wretch had either ſold, or was about to ſell them to the Congreſs.

As the preciſe time in which they ſhould be able to execute their plan could not be aſcertained, it was agreed that Lieutenant Moody ſhould remain at the Ferry-houſe, oppoſite to Philadelphia, till they returned. On going into the houſe, he told the miſtreſs of it, by a conveniant equivocation, that he was an officer of the *Jerſey Brigade*, as he really was, though of that Jerſey Brigade which was in the King's ſervice. The woman underſtood him as ſpeaking of a rebel corps, which was alſo called the Jerſey Brigade. To avoid notice, he pretended to be indiſpoſed; and, going up ſtairs, he threw himſelf upon a bed, and here continued to keep his room, but always awake, and always on the watch. Next morning, about 11 o'clock, he ſaw a man walk haſtily up to the houſe, and overheard him telling ſome perſon he met at the door, that "there was the devil to pay "in Philadelphia; that there had been a plot to "break into the State-houſe, but that one of the "party had betrayed the others; that two were "already taken; and that a party of ſoldiers had "juſt croſſed the river with him, to ſeize their "leader, who was ſaid to be thereabouts." The Lieutenant felt himſelf to be too nearly intereſted in in this intelligence, any longer to keep up the appearance of a ſick man; and, ſeizing his piſtols, he inſtantly ran down ſtairs, and made his eſcape.

He had not got a hundred yards from the houſe when he ſaw the ſoldiers enter it. A ſmall piece of wood lay before him, in which he hoped at leaſt to be out of ſight; and he had ſprung the fence in order to enter it. But it was already lined by a party of horſe, with a view of cutting off his retreat. Thus ſurrounded, all hopes of flight were in vain; and to ſeek for a hiding place, in a clear, open field, ſeemed equally uſeleſs. Drowning perſons are ſaid to catch at ſtraws; with hardly a hope of eſcaping ſo much as a moment longer undiſcovered, he threw himſelf flat on his face in a ditch, which yet ſeemed of all places the leaſt calculated for concealment, for it was without weeds or ſhrubs, and ſo ſhallow, that a quail might be ſeen in it. Once more he had reaſon to moralize on the vanity of all human contrivance and confidence; yet, as Providence ordered it, the improbability of the place proved the means of his ſecurity. He had lain there but a few minutes, when ſix of his purſuers paſſed within ten feet of him, and very diligently examined a thickety part of the ditch that was but a few paces from him. With his piſtols cocked, he kept his eye conſtantly on them, determining, that, as ſoon as he ſaw himſelf to be diſcovered by any one of them, he would inſtantly ſpring up, and ſell his life as dearly as might be;

and, refufing to be taken alive, provoke, and, if poffible, force them to kill him. Once or twice he thought he faw one of the foldiers look at him, and he was on the point of fhooting the man; but reflecting that poffibly though the foldier did *fee*, yet he might have the humanity not to *difcover* him, as he would fain hope was really the cafe, his heart fmote him for his rafh refolution; and he thanks God that he was reftrained from putting it in execution.

From the ditch they went all around the adjacent field; and, as Lieutenant Moody fometimes a little raifed up his head, he faw them frequently running their bayonets into fome fmall ftacks of Indian corn-fodder. This fuggefted to him an idea, that if he could efcape till night, a place they had already explored would be the fecureft fhelter for him. When night came, he got into one of thofe ftacks. The wind was high, which prevented the ruftling of the leaves of the fodder, as he entered, from being heard by the people who were at that time paffing clofe by him into the country, in queft of him. His pofition in this retreat was very uncomfortable, for he could neither fit nor lie down. In this erect pofture, however, he remained two nights and two days, without a morfel of food, for there was no corn on the ftalks, and, which was infinitely more intolerable, without drink. He muft not relate,

H for

for reaſons which may be eaſily imagined, what became of him immediately after his coming out of this uneaſy priſon ; but he will venture to inform the reader, that, on the fifth night after his elopement from the Ferry-houſe, he ſearched the banks of the Delaware till he had the good fortune to meet with a ſmall boat. Into this he jumped ; and having waited a little for the tide of flood, which was near, he puſhed off, and rowed a conſiderable way up the river. During this voyage he was ſeveral times accoſted by people on the water ; but, having often found the benefit of putting on a fearleſs air, he endeavoured to anſwer them in their own way ; and recollecting fome of the leſs poliſhed phraſes of the gentlemen of the oar, he uſed them pretty liberally ; and thus was ſuffered to paſs on unſuſpected. In due time he left his boat ; and, relying on the aid of Loyaliſts, ſome of whom he knew were every where to be found, he went into a part of the country leaſt known to him, and the leaſt likely for him to have thought of ; and at length, after many circuitous marches, all in the night, and through pathleſs courſes, in about five days, he once more arrived ſafe in New York.

All theſe efforts for life were dictated, it would ſeem, rather by inſtinct than reaſon ; for, occupied as his mind had been with his own danger, and his own ſufferings, he can truly ſay, his greateſt uneaſineſs was on account of his brother. There was not a ray of hope that he could eſcape, and leſs, if poſſible, that he would be pardoned. He was the ſon of his old age to a moſt worthy and beloved father, who had himſelf been a ſoldier, and who loved and honoured the profeſſion. Indeed he was a moſt amiable young man, as remarkable for the ſweetneſs of his diſpoſition as for his undaunted intrepidity. Excellent youth! Every feeling heart will forgive the tear which is now dropped to thy memory, by thy ſorrowing brother! He periſhed by an ignominious death, in the 23d year of his age; the news of which, as may naturally be ſuppoſed, well nigh brought the grey hairs of a venerable father with ſorrow to the grave. It did not indeed immediately coſt him his life, but it coſt him, what is more valuable—his reaſon!

His fellow-priſoner was alſo ſentenced to death; but, on making ſome pretended diſcoveries, of no conſiderable moment, he was reprieved. Lieutenant Moody is ſenſible it contains no information that can intereſt the reader; yet, as he preſerves it as a precious *relic*, he perſuades himſelf every man who is a brother will forgive his inſerting an extract or two from his brother's laſt letter, dated November 12, 1781, from the *New Gaol Dungeon, Philadelphia.*

" Dear brother,

" Let me intreat you not to grieve at my fate,
" and the fate of my brother-ſoldier. Betrayed by
" the man on whom we depended to execute the
" plan propoſed by Captain Beckwith, we were
" taken up as *ſpies*; and have been tried and con-
" demned, and are to die to-morrow. I pray you
" to forgive him, as I do, and Laurence Marr
" alſo, as freely as we hope to be forgiven by our
" Maker.—One more requeſt I have to make to
" you is, that, taking warning by my fate, you
" will not hereafter ſo often venture yourſelf out
" of the Britiſh lines. I am in irons; but, thanks
" to the Almighty, I ſtill have the liberty of
" thought and ſpeech. O! may I make a good
" uſe of them, and be prepared, as I ought to be,
" for eternity! Sentence has not been paſſed on
" us above two hours, all which time I have em-
" ployed in prayer, as I will continue to do to the
" laſt moment; and, I bleſs God, I feel quite
" cheerful."

Lieutenant Moody cannot in juſtice cloſe this plain and artleſs narrative, already ſpun out to too great a length, without bearing his public teſtimony, feeble as it may be, in favour of, and returning his thanks, as he now moſt cordially does, to thoſe brave, loyal Americans, whom, though in the ranks only, he ſhall always think it the greateſt honour of his life to have commanded in theſe expeditions. They were, in general, men of ſome property; and, without a ſingle exception, men of principle. They fought for what appeared to be the true intereſt of their country, as well as to regain their little plantations, and to live in peace under a conſtitution, which they knew by experience to be auſpicious to their happineſs. Their conduct in their new profeſſion, as ſoldiers, verifies their character; they have been brave, and they have been humane. Their honeſty and honour have been uniformly conſpicuous. It was a firſt principle, in all their excurſions, never to make war againſt private property; and this has been religiouſly obſerved. Some ſtriking inſtances of their forbearance might be given, if neceſſary, even when they have been provoked to retaliate by private wrongs and perſonal inſults.

And here it ought to be mentioned, with the utmoſt gratitude and pleaſure, that, though Mr. Moody, in the courſe of his adventures, was often obliged to put his life into the hands of the Loyaliſts, in different parts of the country, he never was diſappointed or deceived by any of them. In the year 1777, he continued among them more than three months at a time, and near as long in 1778. He knew their characters, and could ſafely confide in them. They were men of ſuch inflexible attachment to Government, that no temptations could induce them to betray their truſt. Though many of them were reduced to indigence and diſtreſs, and they knew that almoſt any price might be be obtained for giving up ſo obnoxious a perſon, yet they were ſo far from betraying him, that they often ran great hazards in giving him aſſiſtance. Surely ſuch merit as this is worthy of eſteem and admiration; and it is humbly hoped, that the many thouſands in the colonies who poſſeſs it, will not be deſerted by Government, and conſigned over to ruin and wretchedneſs, without an *abſolute neceſſity*.

It is with the utmoſt concern Mr. Moody has heard of the doubts and debates that have been agitated in England concerning the number and the zeal of the Loyaliſts in America. It might be uncharitable, and poſſibly unjuſt, to ſay, that every man who has entertained ſuch doubts, has ſome ſiniſter purpoſes to ſerve by them; but it would be blindneſs in the extreme not to ſee, that they were firſt raiſed by men who had other objects at heart than the intereſts of their country. Men who have performed their own duty feebly or falſely, naturally ſeek to excuſe themſelves by throwing the blame upon others. It would ill become an obſcure individual to obtrude his opinion upon others; but any honeſt man *may*, and, when he thinks it would ſerve his country, *ſhould*, relate what he has ſeen. The writer of this narrative has already diſclaimed all pretenſions to any extraordinary ſhare of political ſagacity; but he has common ſenſe—he can ſee, and he can hear. He has had more opportunities than moſt men of

ſeeing

ſeeing and hearing the true ſtate of loyalty in the *middle* colonies ; and he moſt ſolemnly declares it to be his opinion, that a very great majority of the people there are at this time loyal, and would ſtill do and ſuffer almoſt any thing, rather than remain under the tyranny of their preſent rulers. Let but the war be undertaken and conducted on ſome *plan*, and with ſome ſpirit ; let but commanders be employed who will encourage their ſervices, and leave them under no apprehenſions of being deſerted and betrayed ; and *then*, if they do not exert themſelves, and very effectually, let every advocate they have had, or may have, be reprobated as a fool or a knave, or both together—and let the Americans continue to feel the worſt puniſhment their worſt enemies can wiſh them—nominal independency, but real ſlavery.

Perhaps the honeſt indignation of the Writer may have carried him too far ; but, on ſuch a ſubject, who, in *his* circumſtances, could ſpeak coolly, and with any temper ? That he ſpeaks only what he really thinks, no man, who is acquainted with him, will doubt ; and if, after all, he is miſtaken, he errs with more and better opportunities of being right, than almoſt any other perſon has ever had. He has given the ſtrongeſt proofs of his ſincerity : he has ſacrificed his all ; and, little as it may be thought by others, it was enough for him, and he was contented with it. He made this ſacrifice, becauſe he ſincerely believed what he declares and profeſſes. If the ſame were to do over again, he would again as cheerfully make the ſame ſacrifice. He truſts, therefore, it will not be deemed preſumptuous in him to ſay, that he cannot decently be contradicted in theſe matters by any man, who has neither had ſuch opportunities of informing his judgment, nor given ſuch unequivocal proofs of his ſincerity. The Writer has certainly no bye-ends to ſerve; he is not an ambitious man, nor avaricious. The profeſſion of arms is foreign from the habits of one who has lived, and wiſhes only to live, in quiet, under his own vine and his own fig-tree; and he can truly ſay, that, if his Sovereign ſhould be graciouſly pleaſed to confer on him the higheſt military honours, he would moſt gladly forego them all to be once more re-inſtated in his own farm, with his wife and children around him, as he was ſeven years ago.

He has hitherto received but a very trifling compenſation * for his ſervices and ſufferings; and he looks for no more than will free him from indi-

* During the firſt year he ſerved for nothing, not having the leaſt thought of becoming a ſoldier, or the leaſt doubt of General Howe's ſuppreſſing the rebellion long before the end of it. In the ſecond, third and fourth, he received pay as Enſign; and in the fifth, as Lieutenant. Beſide his pay, upon his taking the firſt mail, he received one hundred guineas, which he divided equally with his three aſſociates. Upon his taking the ſecond mail, he received two hundred guineas, one hundred of which was for himſelf. And this was the whole of what he ever received—except thirty guineas advanced to him by General Robertſon, in order to fit him out for the expedition for the taking of Governor Livingſton. He does not mention twenty-two guineas he has received here in England, becauſe that was merely to pay a bill of charges incurred in one of his expeditions.

gence,

gence, and enable him more effectually to ſerve his country. In enliſting and paying men for public ſervices, he has expended what was ſaved from the wreck of his own fortune to a conſiderable amount, and he was reduced to the neceſſity of borrowing from thoſe, whoſe better circumſtances enabled them, and whoſe generous ſpirits diſpoſed them, to hazard ſomething in the cauſe of their country. This may be called *enthuſiaſm*; be it ſo.—Mr. Moody will not conceal his wiſh, that the world abounded with ſuch enthuſiaſts. Not his fortune only, but his conſtitution, has been greatly impaired by the exertions he has made. His phyſicians re commended a ſea-voyage, a change of air, and a reſpite of his fatigues and anxiety of mind, as the only remedies left him; and the late Commander in Chief, Sir Henry Clinton, was pleaſed to ſecond their recommendation, by politely inviting him to England. He acknowledges, with gratitude, that their kind intentions with regard to his *health* have not been wholly fruſtrated. He truſts he ſhall ſoon be able, and he would rejoice to be called *by the ſervice*, to return to America. He would go with recruited ſpirits, and unabated ardour; for, rather than outlive the freedom of his country, it is his reſolution, with King William of glorious memory, even *to die in the laſt ditch*.

Wardour-ſtreet, N° 97.
Nov. 1782.

JAMES MOODY.

APPENDIX.

The following *Certificates*, ſelected from a great number of others in the Author's Poſſeſſion, are preſumed to be ſufficient to eſtabliſh the truth of his *Narrative*.

N° I.

THE events related in the following Narrative are ſo very extraordinary, that many Gentlemen, who are unacquainted with the country, and with the ſeveral circumſtances, might doubt of the truth of them. I think it therefore a piece of juſtice due to the merit of Mr. Moody's ſervices, to declare, that I believe this Narrative to be a true account of his proceedings.

W^M FRANKLIN,
late Governor of New Jerſey.

N° II.

I DO hereby certify, that Mr. James Moody came within the Britiſh lines in April 1777, and brought in with him upwards of ſeventy men, all of whom, except four, entered into my brigade: That in June following he was ſent into the rebel country for the purpoſe of enliſting men for his Majeſty's ſervice, with orders to continue there until a favourable opportunity offered for him to diſarm the rebels, and arm the loyaliſts, and, with what men he could collect, to join the Royal army; but he was prevented from putting that plan into

into execution, by our army's taking a different route from what was expected: That Mr. Moody, being thus disappointed, assisted by two of his neighbours, soon after embodied about an hundred men, with whom he attempted to join the British army, but was unsuccessful: That afterwards he made two successful excursions into the rebel country, and brought with him from Sussex County about sixty able-bodied recruits, nearly all of whom entered into my brigade: That, after this time, he made many trips into New Jersey and Pennsylvania, and brought in with him many good men, and gained many articles of important intelligence, concerning the movements of Colonel Butler, the real state of the rebel country, the situation and condition of the rebel armies under the command of their Generals Washington, Sullivan, &c: And, that while Mr. Moody was under my immediate direction, he also destroyed a considerable magazine of stores near Black Point, taking prisoners two Colonels, one Major, and several other officers, and broke open the Sussex County jail, rescuing a number of loyalists that were imprisoned in it, one of whom was under sentence of death; besides performing many other important services.

I do also certify, that, in the month of October 1777, the said Mr. Moody was mustered as an Ensign, but received no pay as such till April 1778: That he continued his exertions under my direction till 1780, about which time he was taken from the regiment, which prevented his being appointed to a company in it, as it was in general believed the Commander in Chief intended doing something better for him: That I have every reason to believe Mr. Moody received nothing from government to reward him for his extraordinary

dinary ſervices, or to indemnify him for his extraordinary expences, till 1780: That from the time of his joining the army in April 1777, till his departure for Europe in May 1782, he did, upon every occaſion, exert himſelf with the utmoſt zeal in ſupport of his Majeſty's cauſe in America: And, on the whole, that I believe all that is related in his printed Narrative to be true, without exaggeration.

London, January 30th, 1783.

CORTLAND SKINNER,
Brig[r] General, &c.

N° III.

I DO hereby certify, that during the time I was Commandant of New York, Mr. James Moody went ſundry times into the rebel country, to gain intelligence of the ſituation and circumſtances of the rebels: That at one time he was abſent five weeks in different parts of Pennſylvania and New Jerſey; and brought authentic and full information of the ſituation and reſources of the ſeveral detachments of the rebel army under the command of the Generals Waſhington and Gates, in the year 1779; and the proſpect the rebels had at that time of procuring a loan from France.

That in each of his excurſions he obtained, and regularly reported to me, very accurate information of the rebel country, and appeared to be very zealous and attentive in promoting his Majeſty's ſervice; and from the knowledge I have of his ſervices and ſufferings, I cannot but recommend him as a perſon who merits encouragement and ſupport from the Britiſh Government.

JA[s] PATTISON,
Major General.

APPENDIX.

N° IV.

New York, May 11th, 1782.

LIeutenant James Moody, of the firſt batallion of Brigadier General Skinner's Brigade of Provincial troops, having applied to me for a Certificate of ſome particular ſervices which he has rendered in America; and which, from their having been attempted and in a great meaſure executed during General Knyphauſen's having the command within this diſtrict, I feel much ſatisfaction in complying with the requeſt of this Gentleman, and in expreſſing that Lieutenant Moody, in two inſtances in particular, conducted two ſmall parties, one to Jerſey and the other to Philadelphia, with much perſonal riſk, great ſpirit, and good conduct; and I ever found him deſirous of manifeſting his zeal for the good of the King's ſervice.

GEO. BECKWITH,
Major in the Army,
Aid-de-Camp to his Excellency
General Knyphauſen.

N° V.

New York, May 10th, 1782.

BY ſerving in different public departments in the army in North America, under the command of his Excellency Sir Henry Clinton, I have had opportunities of knowing of ſeveral military exploits, very eſſential and contributory to his Majeſty's ſervice, being performed by Lieutenant James Moody, of the Provincial corps, called the Firſt Batallion of New Jerſey Volunteers, in the execution

cution of which, he not only underwent the moſt ſevere hardſhips, but encountered almoſt every poſſible riſque of his life, as well from theſe hardſhips (which naturally affected his conſtitution), as from the enemy. He however perſevered, in defiance of every obſtacle, with ſuch an ardour and reſolution, as plainly evinced an uncommon zeal and attachment to his King and Country.

STEP. P. ADYE,
D. Judge Advocate.

N° VI.

New York, 11th May 1782.

I THE Subſcriber, do hereby certify, That ſhortly after Major General Pattiſon was appointed Commandant of New York, and I was employed as his ſecretary, Lieutenant James Moody, of the Firſt Batallion, New Jerſey Volunteers, having returned from the country, where he had been engaged in collecting intelligence, &c. appeared at the Commandant's Office, and communicated to me, for the information of General Pattiſon, a variety of accounts relative to the ſituation of the rebel army, &c. which I laid before the General.

From this time an intimacy commenced between us; and Mr. Moody afterwards, previouſly and confidentially conſulted me on the practicability of ſeveral excurſions, he intended to make in the rebel country; and particularly with reſpect to his intention to make Governor Livingſton a priſoner. Mentioning his want of caſh to carry into execution ſo eſſential a ſervice, I offered to ſupply him with twenty-five guineas for this purpoſe, and to be his ſecurity, or to borrow at intereſt a larger ſum, it being out of my power to advance more; but being ſupplied with money by his Excellency Lieutenant General Robertſon, he was enabled to

go

go out without my aſſiſtance. Mr. Moody's failing in this attempt, was owing to one of his party being taken; by which means Mr. Livingſton diſcovered Mr. Moody's being out, took the alarm, and raiſed the country; and with difficulty Mr. Moody eſcaped falling into his hands: but was afterwards unfortunately taken by a party of rebels, and carried to the provoſt-guard at Mr. Waſhington's Head-Quarters, where he was confined, and from whence he made his eſcape, and returned to New York.

Mr. Moody afterwards made various excurſions into the country, and many miles without the Britiſh lines; took ſeveral rebel mails, containing intelligence of great importance, and brought them ſafe to New York. In theſe excurſions he run great riſques of falling into the hands of the rebels, and his health was much expoſed from lying many nights and days in woods and ſwamps to avoid a diſcovery. In theſe excurſions, Mr. Moody diſregarded either the ſeaſons, the fatigue, or the riſques he run.

And on the whole of his conduct, I have every reaſon to believe him intirely diſintereſted, and actuated only by that zeal for his Majeſty's ſervice which he has on every occaſion exhibited.—From Mr. Moody's declaration, and other evidence, I have every reaſon to believe, that the compenſations he has from time to time received, were by no means adequate to the expenſes incurred on theſe occaſions. And I know that Mr. Moody has, at his own expence and credit, ſupported thoſe, whoſe health from a participation of toil and fatigue with him, on theſe excurſions, have been impaired.

John L. C. Roome,
Secretary to Major General Pattiſon,
late Commandant of New York, &c.

7

APPENDIX.

N° VII.

Extract of a Letter from the Rev. Mr. *Brown* (a very respectable Clergyman of New Jersey, now in New York), to the Rev. Dr. Chandler, dated May 10th, 1782.

" YOU will receive Mr. Moody as my particular friend, and as one most firmly attached to his Majesty, and the constitution both in church and state. He has both done and suffered great things from a principle of loyalty. You may give full credit to all he says, and if he tells you some things seemingly incredible, still you are to believe him. He is honest, sober, and firm—never intimidated by danger, and of undeviating probity and honour."

Extract of a Letter from the Rev. Dr. *Inglis*, Rector of New York, to the same person, dated May 11th, 1782.

" MR. Moody is one of the most active partizans we have, and perhaps has run more risque than any other man during the war. He has brought in three rebel mails, and has often been in the greatest perils among false brethren. The history of his adventures will entertain and astonish you. He goes home at Sir Henry Clinton's desire, who has promised to do something for him adequate to his services."

In justice to Mr. Moody, I think it my duty to furnish him with the above *extracts*.

August 23d, 1782.

T. B. CHANDLER.

FINIS.

AUTHOR'S NOTES.

P. 8. [b] Was not the taking Arms againſt the King, at leaſt as high Treaſon, as the fighting againſt their new formd ſelf created States? Yet our Generals ſuffered theſe Executions of the Loyaliſts to go on; without ever attempting to put a ſtop to them by threatening to Retaliate. Nay they would not permit the aſſociated Loyaliſts to ſave their Friends, by threatening to Execute any of thoſe Rebels, whom theſe Loyaliſts had taken priſoners, and whom they then held in their own Cuſtody.

P. 42. [a] A few days after this Genl. Clinton told him, that the Letters were of great conſequence, that the taking of them was a moſt important ſervice. But that he had now done enough; that he would not ſuffer him to venture himſelf in any more of ſuch hazardous Enterpriſes; and that he would take care to provide for him. Mr. Moody does not doubt but that he then intended it; but theſe and his other Intentions ſeldom laſted longer than the day.

P. 50, line 10. He rowed up to Philadelphia: The place from which his purſuers firſt ſate out in ſearch of him; and which he concluded would therfore be the laſt, in which they would look for him.

P. 8, foot. † This was to the fatal Cheaſapeak expedition, to betray the Loyaliſts and to ruin Burgoign.